Original title:
Broken but Whole

Copyright © 2024 Swan Charm
All rights reserved.

Author: Olivia Oja
ISBN HARDBACK: 978-9916-79-254-4
ISBN PAPERBACK: 978-9916-79-255-1
ISBN EBOOK: 978-9916-79-256-8

Whispered Words of Healing

In the stillness, a voice does call,
Soft and gentle, rising above all.
Hearts in turmoil, seeking the light,
Whispered words to restore their sight.

Hands that reach through shadows cast,
Offering solace, peace unsurpassed.
In the sacred, the spirit can mend,
Infinite love, a faithful friend.

Through the valleys, hope springs anew,
In quiet moments, faith shines through.
A balm for wounds, both seen and raw,
In whispered prayers, we find the law.

In the journey, we learn to share,
The burdens lifted, answered prayer.
Beneath the heavens, we find our way,
With whispered words to guide each day.

The Quiet Strength of the Cracked

In the silence, cracks appear wide,
Yet through the breaks, hope will not hide.
Beauty rests where shadows collide,
In the broken, the strength of pride.

From every fragment, stories unfold,
Of trials endured, and hearts made bold.
Resilience whispers through every scar,
For in the cracked, we shine like stars.

Tender moments of grace abound,
In the fissures, love can be found.
The wisdom gained from each weary stride,
In the quiet, we let heaven guide.

Though the world may see only the flaws,
Within each crack, the spirit draws.
Strength emerges from the place we lack,
In the quiet strength of the cracked.

Reverence in Ruins

In the shadows where whispers dwell,
Faith lingers on, a sacred shell.
Amidst the stones, we seek the light,
In broken places, souls take flight.

Glimmers of hope, like stars, arise,
Restoring grace to weary skies.
In every crack, a story sings,
Of love and loss, and what life brings.

Mend Your Spirit

Gather your shards, let them reflect,
A spirit mended, no need to defect.
Through trials faced, find strength anew,
In every storm, His love shines through.

Whispers of mercy, soft and clear,
Guide the lost, calm every fear.
In prayerful moments, hearts align,
A journey back to trust divine.

In the Cradle of Dissonance

Where discord reigns, and chaos roams,
Hearts cry out for sacred homes.
In the cradle of dissonance,
We find our peace in stillness' dance.

Voices clash, yet harmony is near,
In seeking truth, we persevere.
Through trials vast, in shadows cast,
Faith's gentle hand leads us at last.

Sacred Scars

Beneath the surface, scars reveal,
The battles fought, the wounds we feel.
Yet in each mark, a story told,
Of faith revived and spirits bold.

These sacred scars, a testament,
Of grace bestowed, of love's intent.
Embrace the past, let healing start,
For brokenness can mend the heart.

Fragments of Faith

In shadows deep, I seek the light,
Whispers of hope, gentle and bright.
Each tiny spark, a guiding star,
Leads me onward, no matter how far.

Through trials faced, my spirit grows,
Embracing grace, in pain it flows.
Each piece of truth, a sacred gem,
In fragments found, I praise again.

O fragile heart, held in His hand,
In faith, I rise, I understand.
Though storms may roar, I'll stand my ground,
In brokenness, His love is found.

With every tear, a prayer is sown,
In stillness, I find I'm not alone.
The journey's path, both steep and wide,
In every step, He is my guide.

So let my heart, in faith, rejoice,
With each breath drawn, I hear His voice.
In fragments stitched, a tapestry,
My soul in peace, forever free.

A Soul's Resurrection

Awake, my heart, from slumber's deep,
In shadows past, the secrets keep.
With every dawn, a chance to rise,
To greet the light, to touch the skies.

From ashes cold, rebirth shall spring,
In brokenness, the angels sing.
A soul reclaimed from darkest night,
In grace's arms, I find my flight.

With every sin and every scar,
A testament of who we are.
In trials faced, we learn to see,
The strength that grows within, set free.

The chains that bound me fall like dust,
In faith alone, I place my trust.
Resurrected, spirit whole,
In love divine, I find my soul.

Through paths unknown, I walk anew,
With every step, His promise true.
In every heartbeat, whispered grace,
A soul revived, in His embrace.

The Beauty of Imperfection

In every crack, a story glows,
The beauty lies where nature flows.
Adorned in flaws, the heart shall sing,
In imperfection, truth takes wing.

With every tear, a lesson learned,
In winding roads, the heart has turned.
Embrace the scars, they mark the way,
In fragile light, we find our stay.

No perfect path, nor flawless grace,
In humble moments, we find our place.
Each broken piece holds beauty rare,
In love's embrace, we're called to care.

So let me hold my heart with pride,
For in my flaws, God's love is wide.
A tapestry, both bright and dark,
In imperfection, we leave our mark.

In every sigh, a whispered prayer,
In all we are, His love lays bare.
Embracing flaws, we rise above,
In every heart, there blooms His love.

Wounds of Grace

In every wound, a tale unfolds,
A story of courage, yet untold.
With every scar, I learn and grow,
In grace's arms, I find the glow.

The heart in pain finds strength anew,
Through trials faced, I've come to view.
With every tear, a healing stream,
In deepest struggles, I chase the dream.

Wounds of grace, they teach the soul,
That brokenness can make us whole.
For even in sorrow, light shines through,
In every shadow, love breaks through.

So let me carry all I bear,
Each struggle rich, each burden rare.
In every grace, my spirit dances,
Through pain's embrace, I find my chances.

The journey winds, with lessons clear,
In every fall, I rise from fear.
In wounds of grace, I find my song,
In sacred trust, I know I belong.

The Saints of Shattered Hope

In the silence, whispers call,
Hearts uplifted, rise from fall.
Every tear a sacred grace,
Each fracture finds a holy place.

Voices echo through the night,
Guiding souls back to the light.
With every wound that truth imparts,
Saints stitched from broken hearts.

Hope reborn through darkest fears,
Shattered dreams draw forth our tears.
In the ruins, faith expands,
Built by love with gentle hands.

In stillness, prayer's embrace,
Finding strength in empty space.
Miracles in ashes found,
Healing grace, our souls unbound.

Beauty Beneath the Damaged Veil

Beneath the tears of yesterday,
Beauty hides, in disarray.
Softly woven through the pain,
Is the promise of the rain.

In shadows cast by long-lost dreams,
Hope flickers in tender beams.
Veils may tear, yet spirits soar,
Beauty dances, evermore.

With every crack, a new design,
Reflections of the Divine.
Shattered pathways, light will weave,
In brokenness, we learn to believe.

Fragments glimmer, swiftly flown,
Yet in sorrow, love is sown.
Through the veil, the light will break,
God of mercy, hearts awake.

Eden Amongst the Ruins

In the midst of shattered soil,
We find the seeds that grace the toil.
Amidst the ashes, gardens bloom,
Eden whispers, dispelling gloom.

Nature's song, rich and deep,
Gives us promise as we weep.
Through the rubble, life will rise,
Hope's sweet song beneath the skies.

In every shadow, light will grow,
As faith takes root, we learn to know.
God's creation, not in vain,
Beauty thrives through every pain.

Even as the ruins stand,
Hearts unite in love's command.
In the broken, we find whole,
Eden cradled in the soul.

Fragments of Faith

In scattered shards of whispered prayers,
We gather hopes through earthly cares.
Each fragment holds a story bright,
A testament, a spark of light.

When doubts arise like winter's chill,
Faith shines through, unwavering will.
Broken pieces, yet aligned,
In every heart, the truth we find.

Elixirs formed from ancient tears,
Quenching thirst, dispelling fears.
Through every loss, a gain appears,
Radiant love that perseveres.

In the rubble, grace abides,
Mending wounds as faith resides.
Each fragment holds a sacred trust,
In God's wisdom, we find our gust.

Seraphic Sorrow

In the stillness of the night,
Whispers of angels take flight,
Tears of light dance on the ground,
In sacred silence, sorrow's found.

Herald of grace in shadows cast,
A longing heart, shadows amassed,
With jeweled wings, they softly sing,
Of hope, of love, and what they bring.

Beneath the stars, a quiet plea,
In every prayer, a search for free,
To lift the weight of earthly care,
And find the solace dwelling there.

Yet sorrow blooms like evening's rose,
In every heart, a tempest grows,
The balance struck between the two,
In seraph's touch, the pain rings true.

With every breath, the spirit sighs,
In losses borne, the soul still tries,
For joy, for peace, in sacred thread,
To weave the light where dreams have bled.

Embracing the Frayed Edges

In the quiet of the dawn's embrace,
Frayed edges worn, we seek His grace,
To heal the wounds of yesterday,
And guide our hearts along the way.

With every flaw, beauty revealed,
In brokenness, our truth unsealed,
The tapestry of life unfolds,
Each thread a story, rich and bold.

Gather the pieces, lost and torn,
In tender hands, new dreams are born,
Together, we stand in the light,
Embracing shadows, banishing night.

The stumble and fall, the rise anew,
In every heart, the love rings true,
For in our struggles, strength we find,
A sacred bond that ties mankind.

So let us bless the frayed and worn,
Like quiet prayers, our souls adorn,
For in the scars, the light still shows,
In courage found, the spirit grows.

Temples Made from Ashes

From ashes rise our sacred temples,
In every heart where strength resembles,
The fires that once burned within,
A testament to where we've been.

In crumbling walls, the whispers call,
Of hope restored, our spirits enthrall,
Each stone a memory, forged in pain,
Yet beauty born from loss remains.

We gather here, where shadows dwell,
To share the tales no tongue can tell,
In unity, our souls ignite,
As phoenixes take to the flight.

Through fragile faith, we stand as one,
For every night, there shines the sun,
In darkness found, our light invokes,
A rising tide that never chokes.

So lift your eyes, embrace the grace,
In every tear, a sacred space,
For temples made from ashes be,
The holy ground of our decree.

A Pilgrimage of Splintered Dreams

On paths unknown, we wander far,
With splintered dreams, a guiding star,
Each step a prayer, each breath a song,
In search of where our hearts belong.

Through valleys low and mountains high,
With weathered hands, we reach the sky,
For every burden that we bear,
Transforms the weight into our prayer.

The road is long, yet grace abounds,
In every heartbeat, truth resounds,
Fragments of hopes, we carry near,
In faith's embrace, we shed our fear.

A journey marked by trials faced,
The spirit's quest, the soul's embrace,
In every shadow, light will gleam,
A pilgrimage of splintered dreams.

So let it be, our voices rise,
In joyful harmony, we shall advise,
For on this road, together we stand,
In unity, with love, hand in hand.

The Light Beyond the Cracks

In shadows deep, a glimmer shines,
A whisper soft, where hope defines.
Through every wound, and every tear,
The light peeks in, casting despair.

The cracks that mar our weary soul,
Can lead us to a sacred goal.
For in the breaks, His grace pours forth,
Renewing life, revealing worth.

Behold the dawn, a sight so bright,
With every crack, comes stronger light.
The broken paths we once did tread,
Are stepping stones, where faith is spread.

Though darkness clings and shadows loom,
In cracks of stone, blooms life in bloom.
Trust in the journey, let it unfold,
For through the cracks, His light is told.

Healing Through Brokenness

In every scar, a tale remains,
Of battles fought, of unseen pains.
Yet in the depths of sorrow's sea,
We find the strength to simply be.

The fragile heart learns to defend,
Through brokenness, our souls transcend.
Each fractured piece, a chance to grow,
In healing grace, the spirit flows.

Embrace the pain, let it transform,
A shattered world can still be warm.
With tender hands, the Lord will mend,
Our broken dreams, He'll surely tend.

In every wound, a lesson lies,
To see the truth beyond the sighs.
Through brokenness, we rise anew,
In faith and love, we find the true.

Echoes of the Divine

In quiet moments, whispers soar,
The echoes of His love, ashore.
They dance like leaves upon the breeze,
And flow through hearts with gentle ease.

In every prayer, a sacred voice,
Reminding us we have a choice.
To listen close, to seek, to find,
The echoes of the Divine, entwined.

Through valleys low and mountains high,
His presence felt, we cannot lie.
In trials faced, His truth is clear,
The echo sings, "I am always near."

A melody of hope resounds,
In every soul where love abounds.
In unity, we rise, we stand,
Echoes of the Divine, so grand.

Songs of the Unhealed

In silence deep, a sorrowed song,
The tunes of hearts where pain belongs.
Each note a cry, a tearful plea,
For healing grace, to set us free.

The unhealed wounds, like shadows loom,
Yet still we yearn to seek the bloom.
In broken chords, our spirits rise,
To find the light behind the lies.

So let the songs of hurt be sung,
For from the dark, new life is sprung.
In every heart, a symphony,
Of hope and love, eternally.

Together lined, in chorus strong,
We lift our voices, where we belong.
For in the pain, a bond is sealed,
In songs of love, the unhealed healed.

The Quiet Richness of Scar Tissue

In silence, wounds do softly heal,
The scars a testament to our ordeal.
With faith, we rise from ashes, renewed,
Each mark a story, a journey pursued.

Beneath the weight of burdens we bear,
God whispers hope in the midnight air.
Scar tissue glimmers in gentle light,
A tapestry woven through darkest night.

From pain emerges a strength so profound,
In every heartbeat, grace can be found.
The quiet richness of scars we embrace,
A reminder of love's unyielding grace.

With every tear, a lesson unfolds,
The wisdom of ages, in silence retold.
In the garden of sorrow, blooms joy,
Through scarred paths, our spirits employ.

So let us honor the wounds we own,
For in our scars, divinity's shown.
Together we heal, hand in hand to tread,
In the quiet richness, it's love that we've fed.

Embers of the Heart

In the still of night, embers glow,
A flicker of faith, the Spirit's flow.
Whispers of hope dance in the dark,
Igniting our souls with each tiny spark.

Through trials faced, our hearts ignite,
With every struggle comes inner light.
The warmth of love, forever embraced,
At the core of our being, divine grace traced.

In quiet moments, we hear the call,
Of a love that lifts, that never lets fall.
Embers of the heart, we nurture and tend,
A sacred flame that will never end.

As shadows loom, we stand as one,
Knowing in truth, we have already won.
United in spirit, we rise from the fight,
Carried by faith towards the purest light.

So gather the embers, feed the fire,
With love as our guide, we shall never tire.
In each glowing heart, a purpose so clear,
The embers of faith, forever held dear.

The Divine in Desolation

Beneath the weight of a weary sky,
In desolation, where spirits sigh.
A flicker of hope sparks in despair,
In the solitude, we find Him there.

Through barren lands, our footsteps tread,
Each shadow cast whispers what's said.
In the stillness, a voice so sweet,
Guides our way with gentle heartbeat.

From ruins rise the seeds of grace,
In desolation, we seek His face.
The broken path leads us homeward still,
With every trial, we bend, we will.

In the wilderness, our hearts expand,
As we reach out, take His hand.
The divine in desolation shows,
That even from darkness, love brightly glows.

So let the storms come, let them rage,
In every moment, we turn the page.
For in the depths of our lonely fight,
We discover divine in the darkest night.

Unraveled, Yet Whole

Threads of our lives, woven tight,
In moments of anguish, we feel the fright.
But gently, we're unraveled by grace,
Finding unity in each fallen place.

In chaos, there lies a strange allure,
A paradox, a promise held pure.
As we break, we learn to repair,
With love's embrace, we're always laid bare.

In our fragments, a beauty unfurls,
Like petals of hope in life's swirling whirls.
Though torn apart, we mend in His light,
Unraveled, yet whole, we shine so bright.

Each piece a memory, a story to share,
In vulnerability, we breathe the air.
Together we gather, in kinship entwined,
In every lost moment, true strength defined.

So cherish your journey, each tear, every ache,
For in being unraveled, new paths we wake.
With hearts open wide, let love freely flow,
For we are unbroken, unraveled, yet whole.

The Holiness of Our Fragments

In every shard, a light does gleam,
A whisper of the sacred dream.
Each broken piece, a story told,
In shattered forms, the grace unfolds.

We gather what we think is lost,
Count every tear, we bear the cost.
Yet from the ruins, blooms arise,
Reflecting truth through sorrowed skies.

In fragments laid upon the ground,
The heartbeat of the holy found.
Embrace the cracks, the chipped displays,
For in the darkness, love still stays.

With every wound, a lesson learned,
From every scar, a heart is burned.
In humility, we find our grace,
And in our flaws, the pure embrace.

Together in this sacred space,
We weave our lives with gentle pace.
The holiness in all we bear,
Transforms the burdens into prayer.

Divine Paradox

In shadows deep, the light does play,
A paradox in night and day.
In silence, voices rise like fire,
Within our hearts, the soul's desire.

The meek shall find the way to reign,
Through loss and love, through joy and pain.
In every tear, the heavens weep,
For in the struggle's depths, we leap.

To live is to embrace the strife,
The sacred dance, the pulse of life.
In joy and sorrow, faith will grow,
For in the seed, the flower's glow.

The greatest strength lies in the weak,
In humble hearts, the truth we seek.
Through paradox, we find our way,
In every night, we'll greet the day.

So let us wander, hand in hand,
Through cosmic shores and shifting sands.
In every breath of doubt or praise,
Divine is found in fractured ways.

Finding God in the Pieces

In every crack, a promise shines,
Within the chaos, love aligns.
In life's great puzzle, parts we lack,
Yet find the whole within what's cracked.

I seek the sacred in the fray,
In every loss, a chance to pray.
The beauty lies within the breach,
God whispers soft, in silence, teach.

Fragments tell us who we are,
Each broken dream, a guiding star.
In shattered forms, the divine plays,
In every shadow, light displays.

Through whispers faint, we hear the call,
In pieces gathered, we stand tall.
Each wound a portal, wide and vast,
Connecting futures with the past.

So let us cherish every scar,
For in the fragments, light's not far.
Finding God in every creak,
In our true selves, the heart will speak.

Surrendered Shards

In brokenness, I shed my pride,
In surrendered shards, my spirit bides.
Each piece a testimony bright,
Of battles fought and won by light.

In every fragment, grace is sown,
In shattered hearts, love's seeds are grown.
With open arms, I face the night,
For in the dark, I find the light.

To let go of the need to hold,
Is to embrace the warmth of gold.
In vulnerability, I thrive,
And through the cracks, I come alive.

For every splinter tells a tale,
Of journeys where my faith won't fail.
In every tear that falls like rain,
The depth of love will break the chain.

So let me celebrate each flaw,
In every shard, a glimpse of awe.
For in surrender, peace is found,
In brokenness, I'm heaven-bound.

Serenity in the Unraveled

In the stillness, faith does rise,
Amid the storms, we lift our eyes.
With whispered prayers, the heart finds peace,
In love's embrace, our troubles cease.

When trials come, we hold on tight,
Guided by grace, we seek the light.
Each tear we shed becomes a seed,
In time, it sprouts—a hopeful creed.

With every breath, we learn to trust,
For in the ash, we find the dust.
A beautiful dance of joy and pain,
Our spirits soar, yet still remain.

The world may quake beneath our feet,
But in His presence, we are complete.
Through faith anew, our souls will mend,
In His great mercy, we transcend.

So let the waves crash, let winds howl,
For in this journey, we shall prowl.
Hand in hand, we walk through strife,
Serenity found, in this sacred life.

Lifted from the Depths

In shadows cast by weary night,
We seek the dawn, a glimmering light.
Through valleys deep where sorrows drown,
His hand extends, lifting us down.

From chains of doubt, we rise and soar,
In love's embrace, we are restored.
With whispered truths, our hearts ignite,
From brokenness, we seek the right.

Each step we take through trials fierce,
His gentle strength, our wounds He pierce.
From depths of despair, we find our way,
A path of grace, where hope shall stay.

In every heartbeat, His promise speaks,
In rugged paths, our spirit peaks.
For every tear, a blessing flows,
In His embrace, our strength He bestows.

Lifted from depths, we walk anew,
In light's sweet glow, we find the true.
As daybreak's promise paints the skies,
With faith, our souls shall surely rise.

The Covenant of Scarred Hearts

In the quiet where spirits weave,
A tapestry of love we believe.
Through scarred hearts, our pain does bind,
A covenant formed, unbroken, kind.

With every trial, our bond grows tight,
Each wound a testament to the fight.
In wounds that bleed, the grace does flow,
From fractured past, a strength we know.

Together we bear each thorny night,
In arms of mercy, we find delight.
Our stories etched in sacred tome,
In shared resilience, we build our home.

Each scar a mark of battles won,
In love's fierce fire, we are one.
With open hearts, we face the storm,
In unity's embrace, we are reborn.

So let them see, our scars declared,
A testament of love, unscared.
For in the depth of our shared plight,
We form a beacon, radiant light.

The Light of Hope Through Darkness

In shadows deep, where fears reside,
The light of hope, our constant guide.
With every heartbeat, we grow strong,
In darkness' grip, we sing our song.

When nights are cold, and spirits dim,
We turn our eyes, our hearts to Him.
For every tear that falls like rain,
A promise blooms amidst the pain.

Through every trial, He leads the way,
In whispered dreams, we find our stay.
With faith aglow, our path made clear,
In darkest hours, we persevere.

A flicker sparks, igniting flames,
In unity, we lift His names.
With hands together, we stand tall,
Through storm and strife, we shall not fall.

For hope, a beacon through the night,
Guides weary souls toward the light.
In every heart, His love ignites,
A sacred truth, through darkest fights.

The Chorus of the Damaged

In shadows deep, they cry out loud,
Fragments of hope beneath a shroud.
With voices weak, yet hearts ablaze,
Their songs of pain resound in praise.

Each tear a story, each wound a hymn,
In brokenness, they find their kin.
Together they rise, from ashes born,
A chorus bright, a new day's dawn.

The altar stands, their fears displayed,
In whispered prayers, their souls conveyed.
With faith unshaken, in night's embrace,
They seek the dawn, the light of grace.

Their burdens shared, in sacred trust,
In every heart, a glimmer must.
Through trials faced, a unity formed,
In love's pure light, their spirits warmed.

So let the echoes of their song,
Remind us all, we still belong.
For in the chorus of the lost,
Is hope reborn, no matter the cost.

The Luminous Fragmentation

In shattered glass, the truth reflects,
Each jagged piece, a path connects.
Within the cracks, the light does seep,
Turning sorrow into secrets deep.

Radiant shards, like stars confined,
Whisper of grace, in love entwined.
Through brokenness, the soul ascends,
A tapestry where light transcends.

Hope flickers bright in every gap,
A sinuous thread that's tangled, wrapped.
With every cut, a lesson learned,
In sacred fire, the spirit burned.

The heart's mosaic, a work divine,
In every flaw, an artful sign.
With faith as glue, the pieces bind,
Unity found in the redefined.

So let the light through fractures break,
A luminous path, for love's sweet sake.
In every scar, a story spun,
A symphony where all are one.

The Path of Sacred Healing

Upon the trail where shadows dwell,
The heart must learn to rise, to swell.
In gentle whispers, grace unfolds,
A sacred call, a truth retold.

With every step, a burden shed,
The spirit mends where hope has bled.
In nature's arms, the soul finds rest,
A calm embrace, in love's behest.

The river flows, its waters clear,
Each drop a prayer to quell the fear.
In cycles vast, the spirit soars,
Beyond the pain, to open doors.

Through trials faced, the heart will bloom,
In sacred light, dispel the gloom.
A journey carved in joy and tears,
Each moment sacred through the years.

So tread this path, with courage strong,
For healing blooms where we belong.
In every scar, a story deep,
And in that story, love's promise keep.

In the Depths of Our Cracks

In the depths where silence clings,
A whisper rises on fragile wings.
Through wounds exposed, our spirits shine,
In brokenness, the sacred line.

Each crack a portal, a light that streams,
Breaking forth from forgotten dreams.
In every fissure, the heart reveals,
A truth that only pain conceals.

With honesty, we claim our scars,
In honesty, we reach for stars.
For every tear, a seed is sown,
Where love awaits, and warmth is known.

So let us gather where shadows play,
To share our burdens, come what may.
For in the depths, together we find,
A tapestry of the intertwined.

And from the cracks, a voice emerges,
A chorus of hope that gently surges.
In every fracture, light will clasp,
In the depths of our cracks, love will grasp.

Healing Waters of the Soul

In the stillness of the night,
A whisper soft and clear,
Healing waters flow with light,
Washing away our fear.

From the springs of grace we drink,
Renewed in spirit's glow,
In the quiet, we will think,
Of blessings we can sow.

With every drop, a promise made,
To nurture and to grow,
In faith's embrace, we're unafraid,
As love begins to flow.

Let the rivers guide us home,
To where our hearts are free,
In the sacred, we will roam,
In joy's infinity.

Together, we will rise anew,
In unity we thrive,
Through healing waters, we break through,
In hope, we come alive.

The Power of the Frayed

In tattered dreams, a strength is born,
From brokenness, we rise,
The weary heart, though worn and torn,
Can still embrace the skies.

With threads of faith, we mend our seams,
A tapestry of light,
In the shadows, love redeems,
Restoring lost delight.

Each story etched within our skin,
Holds wisdom from the past,
In every tear, a chance begins,
To forge a love that lasts.

With open hearts, we fiercely stand,
In faith, we find our way,
Though life may fray, we understand,
We'll face another day.

The power of the frayed inspires,
A journey bold and true,
In every heart, a spark that fires,
To light the path anew.

The Journey Through Darkness

In shadows deep, we find our way,
Through trials we must face,
In silent night, we learn to pray,
And seek the light of grace.

Each step a choice, a whispered fight,
With courage in our soul,
We trust the dawn will bring the light,
And make our spirit whole.

The stars above, like dreams afar,
Guide us through the night,
In darkness, we can be a star,
With faith as our true sight.

The shadows may seem cold and vast,
But hope will find its way,
For every storm must come to pass,
To greet the breaking day.

In the journey, we are forged anew,
Through every tear and fear,
The darkness teaches love so true,
In light, we persevere.

The Heart's Pilgrimage of Hope

With every beat, a path unfolds,
A pilgrimage we walk,
In hope's embrace, our story molds,
Through silence, dreams will talk.

Each step we take, a vow of trust,
In whispers softly shared,
Through valleys deep, through winds of dust,
In love, we are prepared.

The heart, a compass to the divine,
Maps out the road ahead,
In every struggle, lost in time,
New journeys we will tread.

Through trials faced, our spirits soar,
With faith to light the way,
In unity, we are much more,
The hope that guides our stay.

Together, we will lift our song,
In harmony, we climb,
A heart's pilgrimage, forever strong,
To grace beyond all time.

Whispers from the Fractured

In shadows deep, the spirit cries,
A melody in fractured sighs.
Through broken paths, the light will gleam,
In whispered truths, we find our dream.

The heart, a vessel of sacred stain,
Holds love and loss, joy and pain.
Each fissure tells a tale of grace,
In every scar, the truth we face.

The echoes of the past remain,
In silent prayers, we break the chain.
In every shadow, hope will dart,
A whisper's touch awakens the heart.

From scattered pieces, a whole is formed,
In fragile strength, a spirit warmed.
Divine in chaos, beauty dwells,
Through troubled seas, our solace swells.

In the fractured light, we rise anew,
With every step, the path is true.
The sacred whispers call us home,
From broken bones, we dare to roam.

Blessed Anomalies

In every flaw, a gift divine,
A hidden truth in shadowed line.
Blessed anomalies of the soul,
In cracks of clay, the spirit whole.

The outcast voices, soft yet clear,
Sing hymns of hope for those who hear.
In twisted forms, we find our grace,
The sacred dance, a warm embrace.

With open hearts, we gather near,
In all our wounds, the love is sheer.
Each sacred scar, a story told,
In brokenness, the spirit bold.

Through colors lost, a canvas bright,
The splintered faith ignites the night.
Divine in discord, beauty roams,
In our anomalies, we find our homes.

Embracing all that makes us whole,
In fragmented faith, we seek the goal.
For blessed are the hearts that weep,
In sacred silence, our souls we keep.

The Sacred Scars

Oh sacred scars, a map of grace,
In every wound, a holy place.
The stories inked upon our skin,
Reveal the battles fought within.

With each deep mark, a lesson learned,
Through trials faced, our spirits burned.
In fractured moments, wisdom lies,
A journey marked by sun and skies.

In the quiet nights, we seek the light,
The sacred scars, our beacon bright.
Through shadowed valleys, pain refined,
In every tear, our strength defined.

The past, a tapestry of gold,
In every thread, the story told.
With open hearts, we face the storm,
Through sacred scars, we find our form.

In unity, our wounds connect,
In shared embrace, we find respect.
For every scar, a bond we share,
In sacred love, our hearts laid bare.

Embracing the Splintered

We gather in the splintered light,
With open arms, we hold the night.
In every break, a chance to heal,
In fractured truths, our hearts reveal.

The beauty found in broken dreams,
Illuminates the hidden seams.
We dance upon the brittle ground,
In shattered grace, our hope is found.

Through tangled roots, our spirits climb,
In splintered love, we seek the rhyme.
Each wound embraced, a sacred bond,
In every pulse, the light responds.

The path of thorns, a way to grace,
In every stumble, we find our place.
With every trial, our hearts expand,
In embracing all, we take a stand.

Through splintered threads, the fabric weaves,
A tapestry of hope receives.
In light and dark, we find our way,
Embracing the splintered, come what may.

Resurrection of the Heart

In the silence, whispers rise,
Hope ignites like morning skies.
From ashes, our spirits soar,
Love renews forevermore.

In shadows deep, faith we hold,
Stories of the brave retold.
Broken chains and open doors,
Hearts awakened, joy restores.

Through trials, we walk hand in hand,
In unity, forever we stand.
With prayers that tremble and shake,
From despair, new paths we make.

Surrendering fears to the light,
Transforming darkness into bright.
For every tear, a blessing flows,
In the garden, true love grows.

Eternal spring, our souls embrace,
With every dawn, we seek His face.
Resurrection, our hearts unite,
In faith's embrace, we find our sight.

Songs of the Shattered Soul

In the echoes of our pain,
Resonates a tender gain.
Through the cracks, new melodies,
Rise like larks upon the breeze.

Each note, a step toward the light,
Guiding us through endless night.
With every heartbreak, strength we find,
Healing songs that bind the mind.

In sorrow's depth, we learn to sing,
Of joy and love, the glories bring.
In every shard, a story told,
The shattered soul, a heart of gold.

Familiar voices, lost yet near,
In echoes, we hold those dear.
A symphony of grace unfolds,
In brokenness, the truth beholds.

With every tear, an aria bright,
Crafting beauty from the night.
Songs of the broken yet whole,
Lift us towards our lofty goal.

Finding God in the Fractures

In the fissures of our lives,
Divine whispers gently thrive.
Through our hurt and aching doubt,
God's love beckons, guiding routes.

In every fracture, light can gleam,
Lessons woven like a dream.
Our scars tell of battles fought,
In each wound, a lesson taught.

When the heart is torn apart,
Search for Him within the art.
In the pieces, grace does hide,
Lead us forth, with arms spread wide.

In brokenness, we may find,
The sacred path that heals the mind.
In every crack, a chance to see,
The beauty of our unity.

Let not despair take hold of thee,
For in fractures, God we see.
With His love, we rise anew,
In every challenge, hope is true.

The Blessed Imperfection

In the tapestry of our flaws,
Beauty blooms, and love's applause.
Each imperfect thread we weave,
A testament to what we believe.

Through cracks in our fragile clay,
Light flows in, with grace each day.
In every flaw, a chance to shine,
For broken hearts, the divine design.

Celebrate the scars and bends,
In our journey, love transcends.
With open hearts that dare to show,
The blessed paths that help us grow.

In our frailty, strength we find,
Embracing all that life entwined.
Perfection fades; the spirit's glow,
In our truths, the light will flow.

With each stumble, we shall learn,
In grace's fire, our spirits burn.
A symphony of flaws so bright,
In holy love, we find our light.

Echoes of Redemption

In whispers soft, the angels sing,
A tale of hope, a new beginning.
From darkest depths, the spirit's rise,
To seek the light beyond the skies.

Forgiveness found in sacred grace,
With every tear, we find our place.
The road is long, the path is steep,
Yet faith whispers, 'Awake from sleep.'

For every sin, a chance to heal,
In humble hearts, the truth revealed.
The past now fades, the future glows,
Like morning sun that gently flows.

In unity, we stand as one,
A brotherhood beneath the sun.
Together strong, we'll bear our share,
In love and light, we find our care.

With every step, we forge anew,
A journey shared, with skies so blue.
Redemption calls, we heed its plea,
In every breath, we're spirit free.

The Light in Shadows

In shadows deep, where whispers dwell,
The light of hope ignites the shell.
A flicker small, yet fiercely bright,
It guides the weary through the night.

The heart it aches, yet finds its peace,
In moments brief, the troubles cease.
For every doubt, a prayer takes flight,
Transforming dark into the light.

With steadfast faith, we walk the road,
A burden shared, a lighter load.
In trials faced, we learn to trust,
And rise again from ashes' dust.

Though storms may rage and shadows fall,
The spirit's strength will conquer all.
Through valleys low, we find our way,
In every night, awaits the day.

Embrace the dawn, for it will come,
With rays of grace, each heart will hum.
In unity, we find our song,
A melody where we belong.

The Unbreakable Spirit

In every struggle, strength is born,
A spirit fierce, not worn or torn.
Through trials faced, we rise anew,
With courage deep, our hearts break through.

The weight of doubt cannot confine,
For in the dark, the stars will shine.
Emboldened by each whispered prayer,
We find the peace that lingers there.

Though storms may swirl and shadows loom,
The spirit fights to pierce the gloom.
With every breath, resilience grows,
In love's embrace, true purpose flows.

With each ascent, we challenge fate,
In unity, we cultivate.
For in our hearts, a fire burns bright,
An unbreakable spirit, our guiding light.

Together, we shall weave our fate,
In harmony, we celebrate.
Through struggles faced, our voices blend,
An anthem strong that will not end.

Songs of the Wounded Heart

In silent tears, the heart finds song,
A melody where we belong.
Each wound a note, a tale to share,
In harmony, we find the care.

Through aching paths, our voices rise,
In every pain, a lullabies.
For love can heal what time won't mend,
A sacred bond that will not end.

With every breath, our spirits soar,
In songs of hope, we seek for more.
The wounded heart, it learns to sing,
In whispered vows, our souls take wing.

With threads of faith, we weave our fate,
In every scar, we cultivate.
For through the night, the stars will gleam,
A tapestry of love's bright dream.

Embrace the wounds, for they will teach,
The strength to rise, the love to reach.
In every note, a journey told,
In songs of life, our hearts grow bold.

Harmonies of the Lost

In shadows deep, the whispers call,
A melody for one and all.
The lost souls wander, hearts like stone,
Yet find their song; they're not alone.

In quiet grace, their voices rise,
As prayers converge in endless ties.
The heavens weep for those who roam,
With faith restored, they find their home.

Through trials faced and burdens borne,
New harmonies from pain are sworn.
A choir forms with love's embrace,
Uniting hearts in sacred space.

Beneath the stars, a gentle glow,
Reminds the lost they are not low.
For in each strum of hope's sweet thread,
Lies paths to peace, where grace is spread.

So sing aloud, O spirits free,
In lost harmonies, we see.
The music binds us, soul to soul,
In faith's embrace, we find our whole.

The Light of Restoration

In darkness deep, the light appears,
A beacon bright to calm our fears.
With gentle rays, it guides the way,
Restores our hearts to light the day.

From ashes rise, the hopes reborn,
In quiet grace, our spirits worn.
Each step we take, a promise made,
In love's embrace, we will not fade.

O hands of grace, extend to me,
In trials faced, I yearn to see.
The path ahead, though fraught with pain,
Will lead to joy; the loss was gain.

In every tear, a lesson learned,
The fire of faith forever burns.
Through valleys low and mountains high,
Restoration waits; we need not sigh.

With voices raised, we'll sing anew,
A chorus bold, in peace we grew.
For every heart that finds the light,
Restoration shines, forever bright.

God in Our Disarray

In chaos loud, O Lord, we call,
In every shadow, rise through all.
Amidst the storm, our hearts do strain,
Yet in disarray, Your love remains.

With trembling hands, we seek Your face,
In broken dreams, we find our place.
The puzzle pieces scatter wide,
Yet in Your arms, we will abide.

O gentle Savior, hear our plea,
Through trials faced, our faith sets free.
In every wound, a story shared,
In God's embrace, we are prepared.

The echoes loud of doubt and fear,
Yet in that space, You draw us near.
With every cry and silent prayer,
We find You there, O God, so fair.

So through the night, we walk with grace,
In disarray, we find Your space.
For God resides where hearts are bare,
In every chaos, He is there.

Healing the Fractured

In pieces strewn, our hearts lay bare,
Yet hope's sweet whisper fills the air.
Each scar a testament to fight,
With gentle hands, we seek the light.

Beneath the hurt, a seed of grace,
The fractured soul, aware of space.
Through trials faced, our spirits mend,
With love's embrace, our hearts transcend.

For every wound, a lesson learned,
In healing's arms, our souls discern.
The balm of life, each tear does grace,
With every breath, we find our place.

O joy divine, you find a way,
To soothe the souls that drift astray.
In every crack, a light will stream,
Healing the fractured, the heart's sweet dream.

So rise anew, O weary soul,
In faith and love, we shall be whole.
For in the fragility we see,
The power of grace to set us free.

Shards of Grace

In the silence, whispers of light,
Grace dances softly through the night.
Every tear a story untold,
In fragile hearts, love unfolds.

Hope gleams in the eyes of the meek,
In brokenness, the spirit finds its peak.
Gentle hands mend what's been tossed,
From shattered dreams, it's never lost.

Broken fragments, a holy art,
Pieced together, each plays a part.
In the chaos, find the divine,
In every shard, a sacred sign.

Humbled knees upon the ground,
In surrender, true strength is found.
With each heartbeat, a prayer resounds,
In the stillness, grace abounds.

Love's sweet echo fills the air,
In every moment, know you're rare.
Through cracks and crevices, shine bright,
Embrace the shards, embrace the light.

The Alchemy of Fragments

From ashes rise the golden flame,
In broken pieces, find His name.
Transmuted pain to sacred gold,
In the alchemy, a story unfolds.

Lost within the void, we seek,
In whispers soft, the spirit speaks.
Every trial a step towards grace,
In each fracture, find His face.

Hearts of glass, both weak and strong,
In the shattered, we belong.
Through the darkness, love's embrace,
Transforms our sorrow into grace.

May the wounds teach us to see,
The beauty wrapped in mystery.
In our bruises, hope shall spark,
Guiding us through the endless dark.

Each drop of joy, each tear of pain,
In the blend, the spirit gains.
From fragments, life's purpose grows,
In the alchemy, the heart knows.

Hymns from the Wounded Heart

In the silence of my wounded soul,
Faint hymns rise, they make me whole.
Every scar a note, a sigh,
In the symphony of truth, I cry.

With each pulse, a melody flows,
From deep within, the spirit glows.
Through the shadows, songs take flight,
In the darkness, I find the light.

Broken strings, yet still they play,
In each discord, find the way.
Harmony born of pain, so sweet,
In the mess, life's miracle meet.

Let my voice rise from the depth,
In every breath, my heart's adept.
For in the wounds, a song shall rise,
Lifting prayers to the skies.

With every tear, a chorus sings,
In the wounded, redemption clings.
Through loss and grief, we discover art,
Beauty woven in the wounded heart.

Whispers of the Cracked Vessel

In the crevices of my soul,
Whispers weave, and make me whole.
Each crack a story, a tale of grace,
In brokenness, a sacred space.

From shattered dreams, new paths arise,
In the echoes, hear the cries.
A vessel cracked, yet holds the light,
In each fissure, a guiding sight.

With every flaw, the heart beats strong,
In the struggle, we belong.
Whispers flow like gentle streams,
Carving paths through all our dreams.

In fragile forms, the spirit grows,
Through the cracks, true love bestows.
Let our hearts be vessels bare,
In honesty, we find our prayer.

Though we may falter, we stand tall,
In every stumble, we heed the call.
For in each whisper, truth shall meet,
In cracked vessels, love's heartbeat.

Light Through the Broken Glass

In shadows deep, the light breaks through,
A shimmering path, so pure and true.
Each shard reflects a sacred grace,
Illuminating every space.

Through cracks and flaws, His love shines bright,
Guiding souls lost in the night.
A beacon of hope, forever near,
In brokenness, we find Him here.

He gathers all the shattered dreams,
Transforming pain into holy beams.
With every piece, His beauty grows,
In every heart, a new light flows.

The fractures tell a tale divine,
Of mercy flowing through design.
In every cut, a promise stands,
Together we walk, hand in hands.

So let us trust the paths we tread,
For Light arose where fear had led.
Through broken glass, His truth we see,
Revealing love's pure mystery.

Unseen Threads of Redemption

In silence soft, the tapestry weaves,
Threads of mercy, the heart believes.
Though unseen, they bind us tight,
In darkness, they guide with gentle light.

Each choice we make, a knot of grace,
Intertwined in sacred space.
Every sorrow, a thread of gold,
Crafting stories yet untold.

Through trials faced, redemption calls,
In every stumble, His spirit enthralls.
For in brokenness we find our way,
Into His arms, we long to stay.

The hands that mend, the love that knits,
In every heart, His spirit sits.
Let trust and faith be the tools we wield,
To sow the seeds of love revealed.

No thread is lost, no tear in vain,
In each struggle, His love remains.
Unseen hands weave our fate anew,
In every moment, His promise true.

Mosaic of the Mended

Fragments scattered, hearts laid bare,
In brokenness, we learn to care.
Each piece a story, a life once lost,
Together we rise, no matter the cost.

The potter's hands shape what is whole,
Filling the cracks in our very soul.
A mosaic shines with colors bright,
Each chip reflecting love's pure light.

Though once we fell, and felt apart,
He gathers us close, healing the heart.
In our mending, we find our place,
In the beauty of grace, we see His face.

The art of the broken is not despair,
But a testament to love and care.
In unity, we stand and sing,
Of hope restored in everything.

So let us embrace our varied hues,
The shades of our lives, the joys and blues.
In this mosaic, we find our song,
A harmony where we all belong.

The Divine in Our Splinters

In every splinter, a whisper of grace,
A reminder of love, in a weary place.
Each broken shard reflects a truth,
Of faith's resilience, of cherished youth.

We gather the remnants of all we've lost,
In painful moments, we count the cost.
Yet in our scars, the light breaks free,
The divine speaks through our history.

What once was shattered, now forms a whole,
Revealing the beauty that lives in the soul.
Each splinter a vessel of lessons learned,
In darkness, the flame of hope has burned.

We stand amidst splinters, yet choose to grow,
Discovering love in the spaces we know.
Through trials faced, we find our way,
In the heart of struggle, His light will stay.

Embrace the journey, with gentle hands,
For in our brokenness, His promise stands.
The divine holds fast our splintered dreams,
In every crack, His love redeems.

Voices from the Wounded

In shadows deep, their voices call,
Echoes of sorrow, a sacred thrall.
With every tear, a truth unfolds,
In pain, a story gently told.

Hearts that break, yet rise anew,
From ashes, faith ignites the view.
Each wound a mark, a tale of grace,
A testament to love's embrace.

In whispered prayers, they find their strength,
United souls through endless length.
With every cry, a spirit heals,
Hope springs forth, its promise reveals.

Through trials faced, they find the light,
In darkest hours, they hold on tight.
Voices blend in harmony,
A chorus born from agony.

With every step on jagged ground,
In brokenness, their truth is found.
From wounds, they rise, they soar above,
In suffering, they discover love.

The Unfolding of Grace

In quiet moments, grace appears,
Gentle whispers calm our fears.
Like morning dew on leaves so bright,
It turns our darkness into light.

With every heartbeat, love renews,
In trials faced, we find our cues.
Each stumble brings a chance to see,
Unfolding paths to set us free.

Through every storm, our spirits find,
The courage held in hearts entwined.
In brokenness, we gather near,
In shared embrace, we lose our fear.

The journey stretches, twists, and bends,
Yet in the struggle, grace transcends.
With open hands, we meet our fate,
In trusting love, we learn to wait.

For every tear, a seed is sown,
In love's embrace, we'll learn to own.
The grace that flows through every heart,
Unfolds in ways that set apart.

The Heart's Resilience

Amidst the trials, the heart beats strong,
With every challenge, it knows no wrong.
In faith unshaken, it stands tall,
A warrior's spirit, answering the call.

Through tempests fierce, it holds the line,
In shadows cast, its light will shine.
With scars adorned, each mark a claim,
A testament to love's great flame.

In moments dark, it finds its song,
A melody where we all belong.
Through every loss, it learns to rise,
In resilience, the heart defies.

Though storms may rage and skies may weep,
In stillness found, the heart will keep.
For in the struggle, beauty grows,
A garden where the spirit knows.

Nothing can break the heart that seeks,
In whispered truth, it softly speaks.
With every heartbeat, it finds its way,
In love's embrace, it learns to stay.

Beneath the Surface of Pain

Beneath the surface, where shadows play,
Lies a depth of soul that seeks the day.
In aching silence, a whisper grows,
A strength revealed, as the spirit flows.

With every burden, the heart is tried,
Yet through the storm, it will not hide.
In depths of sorrow, a spark ignites,
Hope is born in the darkest nights.

Each wound a teacher, each scar a sign,
In suffering, the heart aligns.
Through trials faced, we glimpse the light,
In darkness held, we seek the bright.

In quiet moments, resilience sings,
A beautiful truth that freedom brings.
Through layers peeled, we find our grace,
Awakening love in every space.

Though pain may dwell, it will not reign,
A gentle whisper calls through the strain.
Beneath the surface of all we bear,
A heart beats strong, in silent prayer.

The Gospel of the Imperfect

In broken vessels, light will shine,
The grace of flaws, a holy sign.
In every crack, a glimpse of Him,
In our weakness, love grows dim.

Forgive myself, for here I stand,
A sinner saved by His kind hand.
Each stumble leads to higher ground,
In every lost, the lost are found.

The heart of God, it beats for me,
In every shame, His mercy free.
Imperfect hands, yet strong we rise,
With faith that reaches for the skies.

We gather pieces of our soul,
In shared struggle, we are whole.
The truth that lies in every tear,
Redeems our faults and calms our fear.

So let us walk in knowing grace,
Embracing all, in His warm embrace.
For in this life, the truth we find,
Is love will help our hearts unwind.

Ascending from the Ashes

From ashes rose a voice so pure,
A spirit bound that must endure.
With every trial, wings take flight,
From darkness breaks the morning light.

In every scar, a story told,
Of battles fought, both brave and bold.
The heart that learns to trust His way,
Will find the strength to face the day.

With faith anew, we rise again,
Transformed by love that knows no end.
The fire burns, yet we still stand,
In His embrace, we take His hand.

Each tear once shed, a seed of hope,
With grace as guide, we learn to cope.
From brokenness, we find our grace,
In every stumble, we find His face.

So let the past be what it will,
In every void, He bends to fill.
Ascending high, on wings of praise,
We find our strength in darkest days.

Grace in Our Weakness

In shadows cast, His light breaks through,
In every flaw, His love renews.
A tender heart, though bruised and bent,
In grace, we find our true content.

When doubts arise and hope does fade,
He lifts us up, our fears allayed.
In gentle whispers, truth is found,
Through every trial, we'll stand our ground.

Our wounds, a pathway to His peace,
In silent moments, His love won't cease.
Sometimes we fall, yet still we stand,
Embraced by strength, His guiding hand.

Each falter leads to deeper grace,
In brokenness, we find His face.
For in our weakness, strength is shown,
A sacred bond, we're never alone.

So let us treasure this gentle flow,
In His embrace, our spirits grow.
In every scar, His love will gleam,
And grace abounds beyond the dream.

Parables of the Disjointed

In stories told of those who stray,
Shattered pieces find their way.
Through tangled paths and roads unknown,
We seek the light to guide us home.

The lost are found, and hearts made whole,
In every fracture, a glimpse of soul.
The twisted fate, a painter's brush,
In chaos blooms a holy hush.

In our disjointed, He is near,
He sees our pain and calms our fear.
Through parables, the truth is spun,
In every battle, we are won.

Embrace the seams that hold us tight,
In every shadow, search for light.
The stumbling feet will learn to dance,
In sacred moments, find romance.

So weave the tales of hearts once lost,
In every burden, learn the cost.
For in the broken, life unfolds,
A journey new for hearts grown bold.

Echoes of the Sacred Divide

In silence speaks the sacred ground,
Where hearts in shadows can be found.
Voices rise through veil and night,
Seeking solace, searching light.

Beneath the arch of stars above,
The whispers weave of hope and love.
A bridge of faith spans every heart,
Though life may tear, we shall not part.

The divide extends, yet grace will flow,
Through cracks of pain, new seeds will grow.
In every trial, a lesson shines,
Divine presence in our designs.

We gather strength from sacred tales,
Through ancient lore our spirit sails.
Together we rise, though shaken ground,
In echoes loud, our strength is found.

So let us walk with humble stride,
Through valleys deep, with faith as guide.
For every echo, strong and clear,
Reminds us love will draw us near.

Prayers Amidst the Pieces

In brokenness, we find the song,
Of souls that yearn, where we belong.
With trembling hands, we lift our plea,
To mend the scars and set us free.

Each piece a story, carved in trust,
In shadowed corners, rise from dust.
With every prayer, a candle's burn,
As hearts unite, for love we yearn.

Amongst the ashes, hope ignites,
In darkest hours, we find the lights.
Together we stand, though torn apart,
Each whispered wish, a healing heart.

With every tear, a river flows,
Through valleys deep, where mercy grows.
In unity, we share the weight,
For prayers abound, and love abates.

In sacred stillness, peace descends,
Amidst the broken, life transcends.
For in each piece, the world we see,
Is stitched with threads of unity.

The Holy Tapestry of Wounds

Thread by thread, our stories meet,
In woven tapestries, bittersweet.
Colors clash, yet blend with grace,
In every wound, a holy space.

From scars emerge the tales of old,
In every crease, a truth unfolds.
With hands held high, we weave our pain,
In sorrow's depth, there's love to gain.

As stories mingle, hearts unite,
Each whispered wound a guiding light.
For in this fabric, holy seams,
We stitch together shattered dreams.

In love's embrace, the threads entwine,
Transforming loss into the divine.
The tapestry speaks of journeys bright,
Binding us close, through darkest night.

So let us honor every tear,
The holy tapestry, we'll share.
For in this weave, we find our place,
In every wound, the touch of grace.

Cradle of the Redeemed

In gentle arms, the lost are found,
The cradle rocks on sacred ground.
With tender grace, we hold their fears,
And through our love, dry bitter tears.

A sacred trust, the healing touch,
With every child of God, so much.
Through weary roads, we walk in peace,
In every heart, our burdens cease.

The warmth of hope, a guiding light,
In darkness deep, shines ever bright.
Together, we sing the songs of grace,
In every smile, the dawn we face.

As angels watch, we gather near,
In the cradle's comfort, shed each fear.
With lifted voices, we shall proclaim,
In every life, there's love to claim.

In this embrace, the world we mend,
The cradle holds, what love can send.
For every soul, redeemed and free,
In gentle arms, we find our plea.

The Prayer of the Torn

In the silence, hearts cry loud,
Seeking solace in the shroud.
Wounds lay bare beneath the light,
We find strength in darkest night.

With each breath, a whispered plea,
Healing grace, our souls set free.
Gathered shards of broken dreams,
We are mended through His seams.

In the stillness, hope takes flight,
Trusting in the sacred light.
Father's arms wide open, vast,
Embrace us as we rise from past.

Each tear shed, a story told,
In His love, we find the gold.
Through the pain, our spirits soar,
In the struggle, we seek more.

Together we weave our prayer,
A tapestry of love and care.
In the heart, a sacred throne,
We are never, ever alone.

Treasures in the Tempest

When the storms of life do rage,
Faith becomes our silent sage.
In the waves, we find the pearl,
A strength within, unfurled.

Every trial a gem to find,
Crafted well by loving hand.
In the tempest, hope does gleam,
Guiding us through darkest dream.

With each gust, a lesson clear,
Trust in love that draws us near.
Hands uplifted, souls unite,
In the shadows, we find light.

Every heartbeat tells a tale,
Of the grace that will not fail.
Treasures hidden in the storm,
In surrender, we transform.

Through the trials, we emerge,
Stronger still, our spirits surge.
Treasures found amidst the pain,
In His love, we break the chain.

Illuminated by Our Struggles

In the night, our souls ignite,
Struggles cast a holy light.
Each burden that we bear today,
Paves the path, a brighter way.

From the ashes, hope does rise,
In our tears, we learn to prize.
Through the fire, hearts align,
In the pain, His love divine.

Every shadow holds a truth,
Wisdom drawn from age of youth.
Illuminated by the strife,
We glimpse the beauty of our life.

Hands joined in a sacred rite,
Carrying the weight of light.
In our struggle, we are known,
In His grace, we've truly grown.

For in trials, we find our core,
Hearts entwined forevermore.
Illuminated, standing tall,
In our weakness, we hear the call.

The Eucharist of the Unwhole

Gathered here, the broken feast,
In our need, we find the least.
In communion, hearts collide,
We discover love's sweet tide.

Loaves of hope and cups of grace,
In our yearning, we embrace.
Every fragment speaks of Him,
In our hunger, life begins.

Though we feel a little less,
In His arms, we find the blessed.
Through the cracks, His light will shine,
In our unwhole, we are divine.

With each blessing, we unite,
In the darkness, we find light.
The Eucharist of souls combined,
In our longing, love defined.

Together we share the balm,
In the storm, we find the calm.
In our sorrow, joy awakes,
In our hearts, the promise breaks.

Hearts That Hold Both Joy and Pain

In valleys low, our spirits cry,
Yet from the depths, we seek the sky.
With every tear, a lesson learned,
In sacred fires, our souls are burned.

From joy's embrace, pain flows like grace,
A dance of shadows, a holy place.
We carry both, a burden shared,
In faith's own light, our wounds are bared.

With open hearts, we dare to dream,
Through trials faced, we hear the theme.
In brokenness, we find our song,
In every struggle, we grow strong.

The journey winds through joy and strife,
An endless quest, a sacred life.
We walk hand in hand, with love anew,
Hearts intertwined, the pain turns true.

In faith, a tapestry is woven,
Of broken threads, yet love is chosen.
The joy we find in trials met,
Is where our souls will never fret.

Pathways of the Fragmented Faith

In the silence, echoes call,
A step forward, yet we stall.
Faith's shadow, a flickering light,
Guides our hearts through endless night.

Many paths are lost in doubt,
Yet hope arises, a soft shout.
Through fractured dreams, we start to mend,
Upon the wheel, our spirits bend.

With every struggle, we might find,
A clearer purpose intertwined.
Each broken piece, a sacred part,
Awakens joy within the heart.

We wander through the fields of prayer,
In quiet moments, we lay bare.
For through the storms, our faith will rise,
A phoenix born from anguished skies.

Together we stand on this ground,
In shattered faith, our hope is found.
The pathways twist, yet we believe,
In unity, our souls perceive.

The Silent Song of the Bruised

In darkened rooms, where whispers fade,
The silent song of pain is made.
Each note a story, softly spun,
Of battles lost, yet battles won.

With heavy hearts, we cradle woes,
In tender grace, the spirit grows.
Through every bruise, a silent prayer,
In hidden corners, faith lays bare.

The harmony of hurt and grace,
Resounds in time, a sacred place.
For when we're broken, spirits soar,
In silence, love unlocks the door.

Though bruised and battered, we still sing,
A melody for the suffering.
In every scar, a glimmer shines,
A testament of love that binds.

Embraced by faith, our wounds reveal,
The silent song, a healing seal.
Each heartbeat echoes, soft and true,
In unity, we start anew.

Shattered Light

Through prisms bright, our dreams take flight,
Yet shadows linger, veiling light.
In shattered pieces, beauty's born,
A canvas rich, where hope is worn.

Each fragment holds a sacred glow,
In every crack, the spirit flows.
We gather light from broken things,
In shattered truth, our spirit sings.

Though darkness comes, we find our way,
A flicker bright in light of day.
For every shard that falls apart,
We rise anew, with open heart.

In fractured spaces, grace appears,
Transforming pain to light through tears.
In every step, the journey bends,
Towards the hope that never ends.

With shattered light, we paint the skies,
A vivid hue that never dies.
In every moment, we unite,
To weave a world of purest light.

The Sacred Dance of Imperfection

In the quiet of night, we sway,
In shadows, we find our way.
The flaws we wear like jeweled crowns,
In humble hearts, love abounds.

Each misstep in the cosmic waltz,
A canvas of the Creator's faults.
Our spirits dance to grace's song,
In our imperfection, we belong.

With every tear, a spark ignites,
A testament of heavenly lights.
In the tapestry of our lives,
Through every wound, divinity thrives.

Embrace the beauty in the scar,
For every soul's a shining star.
In the dance of love, we find our truth,
Through every trial, we renew our youth.

Let the sacred rhythm inspire,
A burning flame, a holy fire.
For in this dance, we become whole,
Perfectly flawed, yet pure in soul.

Threads of Restoration

In the weave of time, we mend,
Broken hearts begin to blend.
With threads of hope, we stitch the night,
Creating warmth, igniting light.

Each tear a mark of sacred grace,
Every distance finds its place.
Through trials faced, we seek to grow,
Restoration in the ebb and flow.

Hands entwined in faithful prayer,
A chorus lifted in the air.
With faith, we gather all that's torn,
In love's embrace, the spirit's born.

Through storms of doubt, we find our ease,
In every challenge, gentle peace.
The threads we weave, a testament,
To love, a force omnipotent.

Together we rise, united strong,
In sacred trust, we carry on.
With every stitch, our spirits soar,
For through restoration, we explore.

Reflections of Grace

In the mirror of the soul, we gaze,
Finding light in the hidden ways.
Each flaw, a reflection of His might,
In humble hearts, we shine so bright.

With every prayer, a whisper flows,
As love within our spirit grows.
In shadows cast, His mercy beams,
Awakening our sacred dreams.

Through every challenge faced each day,
We learn to bend, but never sway.
With grace, we walk the narrow line,
In every fall, His love we find.

As rivers flow with purpose deep,
In gratitude, our hearts will leap.
For every moment, pure and true,
In grace, our lives are made anew.

Let kindness lead and hope inspire,
In every heart, ignite the fire.
For in the dance of love and light,
We find our way through darkest night.

Beauty Amidst the Shambles

In wreckage lies a hidden gem,
A testament of what has been.
Through shattered dreams, we find the grace,
In broken places, love's embrace.

From ashes rise the strength we own,
In chaos, seeds of hope are sown.
With open hearts, we choose to see,
The beauty in our vulnerability.

Each scar a story, each tear a tale,
In every moment, we prevail.
For in the struggle, lives the art,
A masterpiece of the sacred heart.

In every stumble, we are refined,
In life's wild dance, our souls entwined.
Through trials faced, we learn to grow,
In the shambles, love's colors glow.

Let every fragment turn to light,
Drawing us closer to what is right.
For within the mess, redemption waits,
In beauty's arms, we open gates.

The God Who Mends

In the silence, He whispers grace,
Finding hearts lost in their place.
With gentle hands, He starts to weave,
A tapestry of love, we believe.

He sees the cracks, the wounded seams,
Restoring hope, igniting dreams.
With every thread, He pulls us near,
In His embrace, we shed our fear.

From brokenness, new life shall bloom,
In darkened spaces, He lifts the gloom.
For every scar is light in disguise,
The God who mends, He hears our cries.

Through trials faced, His strength is shown,
For in our struggle, we are not alone.
Through storms of doubt, His love withstands,
An everlasting hope in His hands.

Grace in the Ruins

In the rubble where faith has faltered,
Amidst the ashes where dreams once altered,
There lies a promise, tender and true,
A flicker of grace to carry us through.

With every tear, a seed is sown,
In barren places, His love is grown.
The ruins speak of stories untold,
In brokenness, His mercy unfolds.

From every wound, a whisper rises,
A call to hope in dark disguises.
In sacred silence, we find our voice,
Through trials endured, we still rejoice.

For grace abounds where shadows loom,
In fractured paths, His light will bloom.
The ruins echo with melody sweet,
A symphony of faith beneath our feet.

The Tenderness of Splintered Souls

In the depth of hurt, love finds a way,
Healing the splinters of yesterday.
A tender touch on hearts that ache,
In every loss, new bonds we make.

With eyes that see the broken parts,
He crafts the pieces, mending hearts.
In vulnerability, strength unfolds,
A beauty rising, a story told.

Through shared embraces, we learn to heal,
In splintered souls, the wounds are real.
Yet in the fracture, love's light breaks,
A tapestry woven from what fate makes.

The tenderness found in shattered dreams,
Is where the heart learns to sew its seams.
For in each crack, His grace pours down,
A crown of compassion, our hearts renown.

Fractals of Eternity

In the cosmos, His patterns unfold,
In every heartbeat, a story told.
Fractals of grace, an infinite line,
Reflecting His glory, divine and benign.

In every moment, eternity breathes,
The fabric of time, in love it weaves.
With every heartbeat, creation sings,
Fractals of hope in the joy that clings.

As seasons change, His promise remains,
In cycles of life, He breaks our chains.
With eyes of faith, we seek to see,
The fractals of love, our destiny.

In the universe vast, we stand in awe,
In every tear, His beauty we draw.
Through fractals of grace, we learn to soar,
In the heart of the wind, He opens doors.

The Heart's Redemption

In shadows cast by doubt's cruel hand,
A whisper calls from a distant land.
Restoration flows like a gentle stream,
Awakening hope, rekindling dream.

Through trials faced and burdens borne,
A soul once wrecked now starts to mourn.
Each tear a drop of sacred wine,
Pouring forth love's design.

The heart, once heavy, begins to soar,
With faith as wings, it craves for more.
In grace's embrace, we find our way,
Each moment cherished, come what may.

From brokenness, a beauty glows,
In every crack, the light still flows.
Forgiveness blossoms in tender light,
Transforming darkness into bright.

The journey leads to sacred ground,
Where peace and love in union found.
With open hearts, we walk the path,
In redemption's joy, we feel His wrath.

Cracked Vessels

In every crack, a story dwells,
Of broken dreams, of whispered spells.
Yet through the flaws, His glory shines,
Reviving faith in weary signs.

A vessel worn, with scars to show,
Each fissure a place for rivers to flow.
In weakness found, our strength is born,
Transcending heartache, love adorns.

As autumn leaves drift to the ground,
In loss, we find the sacred sound.
The beauty of the imperfect grace,
In every heart, His warm embrace.

From shattered pieces, a new form grows,
A life reborn, as the spirit knows.
With every breath, remembrance sings,
Of hope restored and all it brings.

Thus cracked vessels find their place,
In the tapestry of divine embrace.
In brokenness lies a path so pure,
For all our wounds, our hearts endure.

In the Midst of Ashes

In the depths of despair, where hopes decay,
Amidst the ashes, we kneel and pray.
For every shadow that cloaks the day,
A spark of faith ignites the way.

From charred remains, a new dawn breaks,
In silence we gather, our hearts awake.
The embers whisper of love reborn,
In pain's embrace, the spirit's sworn.

The past may linger in flickers of light,
Yet from the ruins, we rise in might.
The ashes cradle what once was lost,
In resurrection, we count the cost.

Through fire's trial, we are refined,
In the darkest nights, His grace aligned.
The hope of morning, a promise clear,
In the midst of ashes, He draws near.

So let us dance in the smoke's embrace,
For in the ruins, we find His grace.
Each step a prayer, each heart a song,
In the midst of ashes, we grow strong.

The Alchemy of Suffering

In suffering deep, a treasure hides,
Transforming pain where love abides.
Through silent cries and heavy sighs,
We find the gold that never dies.

Each wound a lesson, each trial a gift,
In darkness, spirits begin to lift.
Through tears that fall as the night enfolds,
The alchemy turns our hearts to gold.

In moments when the weight feels more,
We seek the light behind the door.
For in the depths of our weary souls,
God's gentle touch makes broken whole.

Through fire and storm, we learn to see,
The beauty that lies in our history.
For suffering shapes what we become,
In the alchemy of love, we are one.

So let us embrace the trials we face,
For in the dance of grief, we find grace.
Each sorrow whispers what hope can yield,
In suffering's womb, a heart is healed.

The Splintered Journey to Wholeness

In shadows deep, we seek the light,
Our fractured paths in faith unite.
Each step we take brings healing's song,
In His embrace, we all belong.

With every tear, a seed is sown,
From brokenness, the heart has grown.
We wander lost, yet find our way,
In whispered prayers at end of day.

The journey long, but worth the fight,
To glimpse the truth and share the light.
The splintered roads shall guide us home,
To grace where we are not alone.

In every trial, His hands are near,
With love that wipes away our fear.
We gather strength from every fall,
In sacred silence, we hear the call.

A tapestry of scars and dreams,
In unity, our spirit gleams.
So let us walk with heads held high,
In faith we stand; in love we fly.

Prayerful Ruins

Among the stones, where silence dwells,
A heart still beats, and spirit swells.
Each prayer we whisper finds its place,
In ruins, we encounter grace.

The walls may crumble, yet hope remains,
In every crack, a wild refrain.
With every breath, a chance to rise,
To seek the truth beyond the skies.

The echoes of the past do sing,
In moments lost, new dawns take wing.
We gather here, with broken pride,
In prayerful ruins, love our guide.

The stones may tell of battles fought,
In every loss, the wisdom sought.
A sacred place where souls confide,
In ruins, our faith is amplified.

From ashes, we will build anew,
With hearts ablaze, our spirits grew.
For in these ruins, we reclaim,
The sacred truth, in love's sweet name.

The Intersection of Loss and Grace

In twilight's glow, we stand alone,
The weight of loss, a heavy stone.
Yet in the silence, whispers flow,
Of grace that meets us, deep and slow.

The paths we tread are fraught with pain,
Yet through the dark, a hope remains.
In every tear, a lesson found,
In absence full, we stand unbound.

We gather strength from what we miss,
In brokenness, we find our bliss.
For in the void, His presence glows,
A gentle balm where sorrow flows.

We learn to dance in shadows cast,
To cherish moments that have passed.
For every end, a brand new start,
In loss, we find a healing heart.

Together here, we find our place,
At the intersection of loss and grace.
With open hearts, we dare to feel,
In every wound, the power to heal.

The Sacred Embrace of Vulnerability

In gentle hands, our hearts unfold,
In softest whispers, truths are told.
To bare our souls, a daunting task,
Yet in this space, we dare to ask.

For in the cracks, the light does shine,
Through fragile forms, the love divine.
We find our strength in tender cries,
In vulnerability, the spirit flies.

Each scars a tale, a journey shared,
The sacred ties through pain declared.
With open arms, we welcome all,
In pain, we rise; in love, we fall.

The courage found in letting go,
Through honest tears, our spirits grow.
For in the hurt, connection blooms,
In sacred space, our being looms.

So let us dance in our fears today,
In perfect grace, we find our way.
For in this embrace, we are complete,
The sacred truth in vulnerability, sweet.

The Well of Hope

In the stillness of night, we seek,
A whispering light, a gentle peak.
From the depths of despair, we rise,
Drawn to the well, where hope never dies.

With each drop that falls, grace flows free,
Quenching the thirst of souls, we see.
Lifting our spirits, hearts interlace,
In the well of hope, we find our place.

Fear's shadow can loom, but we reach,
The promise of dawn, the lessons it teaches.
In every heartbeat, in each prayer laid,
We gather the strength, in faith we are made.

Sowing seeds of love in barren ground,
With every prayer, a miracle found.
Together we grow, side by side,
In the well of hope, forever abide.

So let us drink deep from this sacred source,
And walk together, in love's pure course.
For in the well, we are never alone,
In the arms of hope, we find our home.

The Tapestry of Pain and Grace

Threads of sorrow intertwine with joy,
A tapestry woven, no true decoy.
In the loom of life, each strand plays its part,
As pain gives birth to grace in the heart.

Stitches of struggle, colors of strife,
Adorn the fabric, the journey of life.
Yet each knot of anguish, each tear that falls,
Becomes a reminder, the grace that calls.

Golden strands of laughter shine through the gray,
While shadows remind us of night's long stay.
In every dark corner, a glimmer we trace,
For in this weaving, we recognize grace.

Love's gentle hand, a weaver so wise,
Brings hope from despair, the truth in our eyes.
Together we rise, through trials embraced,
In the tapestry of pain and grace.

So let us create, with heart open wide,
A masterpiece born from each tear we cried.
For life's a rich fabric, both fragile and strong,
In this gallery of love, we all belong.

A Journey Through the Fractured

In the valley of shadows, we wander alone,
With hearts full of questions, we search for our own.
The path may be broken, the road unclear,
Yet in every fracture, His presence is near.

Through hills of despair and mountains of doubt,
We learn from the quiet, the stillness, and shout.
Each step that we take, though trembling and frail,
Leads us to strength that will never curtail.

The echoes of anguish turn songs into light,
Illuminating the way, restoring our sight.
As we climb through the darkness, our spirits ignite,
With love as our compass, we embrace the night.

Each bruise that we carry becomes part of our song,
A melody of healing, where we truly belong.
In the dance of the fractured, we gather and soar,
For what once tried to shatter makes us whole evermore.

So onward we journey, hand in hand with the frail,
With hearts intertwined, we shall never fail.
For every step taken on this sacred ground,
Is a testament of faith, where love is profound.

Prayers of the Imperfect

With trembling hands, we lift our plea,
In the quiet of night, where we long to be free.
For every fault, every scar that remains,
Is a prayer for mercy, in joy and in pains.

In the chorus of voices, both strong and meek,
We join in unison, hearts that speak.
Bathed in His grace, our burdens we share,
In the prayers of the imperfect, He listens with care.

Each stumble we make, a lesson unfolds,
As our stories are woven, in threads of gold.
With love as our anchor, together we rise,
In the warmth of forgiveness, our spirits fly high.

So let us not fear the cracks of our soul,
For they let in the light, they help make us whole.
In His embrace, we are beautifully flawed,
In the prayers of the imperfect, we're shaped by His love.

With gratitude spoken, we gather and pray,
For strength in our journey, with each passing day.
In unity we stand, in faith we remain,
For in prayers of the imperfect, we find our refrain.

The Spirit's Mosaic

In colors bright the spirit thrives,
Each shard reflects the light of lives.
A tapestry of faith and grace,
In every heart, a sacred space.

Through trials deep and shadows cast,
We find our strength, our love, our past.
With every piece, a story told,
In unity, our hopes unfold.

The pieces scattered, yet so near,
In fragments bright, we conquer fear.
A mosaic formed of joy and strife,
In every crack, the breath of life.

The spirit guides us through the night,
With every step, we seek the light.
Together woven, hand in hand,
In the design of sacred land.

So let us cherish every hue,
For in each soul, the spirit's true.
A masterpiece beyond compare,
In every heart, the spirit's care.

Hope from Ruins

From ashes rise a whisper soft,
In broken dreams, our spirits loft.
Each tear a seed, in soil of pain,
From shattered hopes, new life will gain.

The ruins speak of paths once walked,
In every silence, love has talked.
With every breath, the chance to mend,
In every heart, a hopeful trend.

Let not despair take root and stay,
For dawn shall break with light of day.
In darkest nights, our souls ignite,
A beacon shines, reclaiming sight.

Hope echoes through the barren land,
In every grain, the Maker's hand.
From what is lost, we find our way,
In every sorrow, seeds of play.

So let us stand, united strong,
In faith and love, where we belong.
From ruins rise a grand refrain,
In every heart, hope shields the pain.

Scattered Prayers

Like stars that twinkle in the night,
Our scattered prayers take flight.
Each whispered word, a gentle grace,
In heaven's arms, they find a place.

In quiet moments, hearts align,
With every plea, our spirits shine.
A collective voice, both meek and bold,
In sacred trusts, our stories told.

Through trials faced and burdens shared,
In every prayer, a heart laid bare.
The echoes rise like fragrant smoke,
In every sigh, the love we cloak.

As raindrops fall upon the ground,
In scattered prayers, grace is found.
With every tear and joyful shout,
In unity, we weave about.

So let them soar, our prayers on high,
In faith and hope, they'll never die.
For in each word, a piece of soul,
In scattered prayers, we are whole.

Unseen Wholeness

In every crack, there's beauty found,
In whispered love, a joyful sound.
Though pieces seem to drift apart,
The unseen wholeness fills the heart.

In quiet spaces, grace abounds,
In fragile places, truth surrounds.
We're woven tight, though eyes can't see,
The threads that bind in unity.

With every trial that leaves a mark,
The light shines brighter in the dark.
For in the struggle, strength is born,
Through fractured paths, our hearts are worn.

Amidst the storms, we seek the peace,
In unseen wholeness, love increase.
A sacred dance, both lost and found,
In every heartbeat, hope unbound.

So let us trust in what we know,
In unseen wholeness, we will grow.
For though apart, we are one soul,
In every spirit, a shining goal.

Embrace of the Imperfect

In the canvas of life, flaws take their space,
A divine brush strokes with gentle grace.
Every scar tells a story, a tale of the heart,
Embrace the imperfect as a sacred art.

In shadows we wander, seeking the light,
Each stumble a lesson, a path to insight.
With open hands, we welcome the pain,
For through every thorn, blossoms the gain.

In whispers of night, hear the echoes of trust,
Even broken vessels hold treasures robust.
Each crack is a doorway, a glimpse to embrace,
The beauty of grace in a flawed, tender space.

Let imperfect harmony ring in our souls,
As we dance through the chaos, fulfilling our roles.
In unity found, we rise and we fall,
For the heart sings its truth beyond every wall.

So gather, dear wanderers, join hands in the fray,
Let love be the light that will guide us each day.
In every misstep, find purpose anew,
For in the embrace of the flawed, we are true.

The Harmony of Little Fragments

In the mosaic of life, pieces intertwine,
Fragmented beauty in a grand design.
Each piece finds its place in the sacred whole,
Together they form a divine, living soul.

Like stars in the heavens, scattered afar,
Little fragments shine, illuminating who we are.
In whispers of love, they silently sing,
A testament to hope in each broken thing.

As rivers converge, their waters unite,
From tiny droplets emerges the might.
In our differences, a symphony grows,
Every heartbeat a note that endlessly flows.

Gather the pieces, embrace every hue,
The harmony blossoms in the depths of you.
In the stillness of silence, unity hums,
From the fragments of life, a new journey comes.

So seek out the beauty, the small and the grand,
In the fragments of life, hold the mystery's hand.
Trust in each moment, in the paths we've unfurled,
For together we dance through this wondrous world.

Sacred Lessons from Our Cracks

In the fissures of time, wisdom unfolds,
Lessons are whispered, narratives told.
Each crack a reminder of journeys we've faced,
The sacred truths in our shadows are traced.

In the moments we falter, grace finds its way,
Through trials and pain, the heart learns to sway.
For in brokenness lies a nurturing seed,
The promise of growth from our deepest need.

So gather the lessons born from our scars,
Like constellations guiding us from afar.
In the tapestry woven with laughter and tears,
Find strength in the cracks that conquer our fears.

Embrace every flaw; let it teach you to shine,
For the sacred is found in each line divine.
With every misstep, our souls intertwine,
Crafting a rhythm, a love so sublime.

So walk through the valleys, let courage ignite,
For within every crack, the spirit takes flight.
Trust in the lessons, let them lead the way,
For the sacred resides in the cracks of today.

The Resurrection of the Hollow

In the hollow of silence, the spirit ignites,
Whispers of courage emerge from the nights.
From emptiness springs a delicate grace,
The resurrection unfolds in a sacred space.

Like dawn breaking soft after long, starry hours,
The heart finds its voice amidst withering flowers.
In depths we discover the echoes of light,
Rebirth in the shadows, a glorious sight.

From broken foundations, new dreams take their flight,
Through moments of stillness, the soul finds its might.
Embrace the hollow, for it leads us to whole,
A resurrection of love, transforming the soul.

As the seasons conspire to weave life anew,
The fragile becomes fierce, the ordinary true.
In every lost path, find the threads of the divine,
For in our hollow places, the spirit aligns.

So rise from the ashes, let hope reappear,
In the depths of the hollow, we conquer our fear.
Together we flourish in the warmth of the sun,
For the resurrection of hollow leads to the one.